To my wife, who always helps me find my keys, and sometimes, my marbles.

Text Copyright © 2019 Roy Lieberman.
Illustrations copyright © 2019 Roy Lieberman.
All rights reserved. No part of this book may be reproduced or transmitted in any form or by any means, electronic or mechanical, including photocopying, recording, or by any information storage and retrieval system, without written permission from the author.

First edition 2019

The illustrations in this book were rendered in black ink pen and watercolors.

Library of Congress Cataloging-in-Publication Data, Lieberman, Roy
Relay / Written by Roy Lieberman; Illustrated by Roy Lieberman - 1st ed.

Coolidge Corner Press
175 Freeman St., Brookline, Massachusetts 02446
editor@coolidge-corner-press.com

Printed in the USA
ISBN: 978-1-7338376-1-3
[1. Transportation - Fiction. 2. Vehicles - Fiction. 3. Machinery - Fiction.]
10 9 8 7 6 5 4 3 2 1

RELAY

by Roy Lieberman

Coolidge Corner Press
Brookline

That morning, Dad lost his car keys. *Again*.

"Russ, Ben, have you been playing with my keys?" asked Dad. "I can't find them anywhere."
"Only babies play with keys!" said Ben before knocking over his glass by mistake.

I turned around and smiled. "Actually, a strange buzzing sound did wake me up last night."

"Oh, really?" Dad raised an eyebrow. "You didn't happen to see what was making the noise, did you?"

I nodded. "I snuck out of bed and couldn't believe my eyes! A small blimp was floating next to the staircase as if checking that everyone was fast asleep."

"Russ, this wouldn't be like the time you told me aliens put my slippers in the dishwasher, would it?"
"Nope. The blimp squeezed out the hallway window and floated away."
"Good!" said Dad.

"Looking closer, I saw tiny people making the machines go! One machine opened the cabinet drawer and another machine grabbed your keys and yanked them out!"

Dad and Ben were looking at me with wide eyes, but since they were quiet, I continued.

"Next, the keys were dropped into the bed of a yellow truck that drove them to the edge of the cabinet. A cable car was waiting to give them a ride to the floor."

"At the bottom, they were secured to the back of a 34-wheel crane to prepare for the long haul up the stairs."

"You're right, Ben, it can't." I paused for a second. "That's why the crane loaded the keys onto a three-legged machine when it got to the staircase."

"Step by step it climbed, carefully moving one leg at a time so the keys wouldn't fall."

"At the top of the stairs, a forklift picked up the keys and carried them to the bathroom.
"I prayed that they were not headed for the toilet."

"Ha ha," Ben laughed. "The keys are in the toilet!"

"Nope." I said. "They went the other direction to a tall elevator machine that lifted the keys all the way up to the bathroom countertop."

"A digger scooped up the keys and began to push them towards the sink."

"Ha ha, the keys went down the drain!" laughed Ben.

"Would you stop interrupting?" I cried. "They didn't fall into the sink! The shovel went right past it, to the very edge of the counter, and with one final push, down fell the keys,

straight...

into...

the laundry basket!"

Dad jumped up, like toast from a toaster and rushed upstairs. **"Found them!"** he shouted from across the house.

When Dad came back, he hugged me tightly and said, "I'm glad you saw the 'relay race' that happened here last night.

"Only next time," he whispered into my ear, "can the story be a tiny bit shorter?"

As Dad zoomed off to find the shoe he lost on his way up, Ben turned to me with a funny look.

"Ruuuuuuuss," he said. "Did all that stuff really happen?"

"It might've." I shrugged my shoulders. "Either way, I bet Dad will stop leaving his keys in his pants from now on!"

About the Author

When Roy was in the second grade, he used to daydream about fantastical machines that could do extraordinary feats - cranes that could lift entire cities, dinosaur-like contraptions that could tame a tornado, and huge bulldozers capable of pushing mountains aside.

"No good will come from daydreaming," his teachers told him. "Unless, that is, you would go on to write a children's book one day."

And that's exactly what happened.

www.ingramcontent.com/pod-product-compliance
Lightning Source LLC
LaVergne TN
LVHW072058070426
835508LV00002B/151